# At the Party

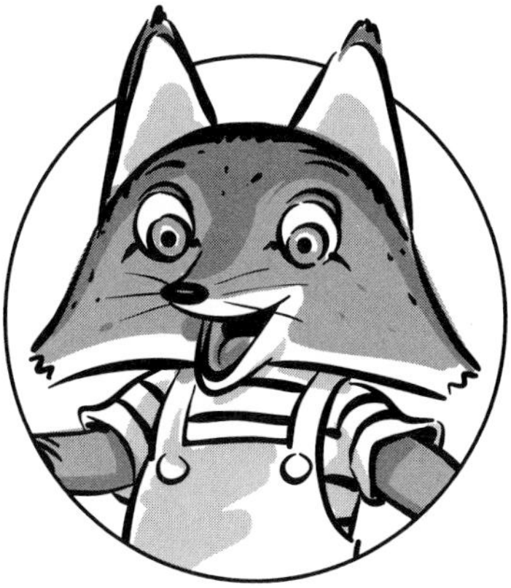

HOUGHTON MIFFLIN BOSTON

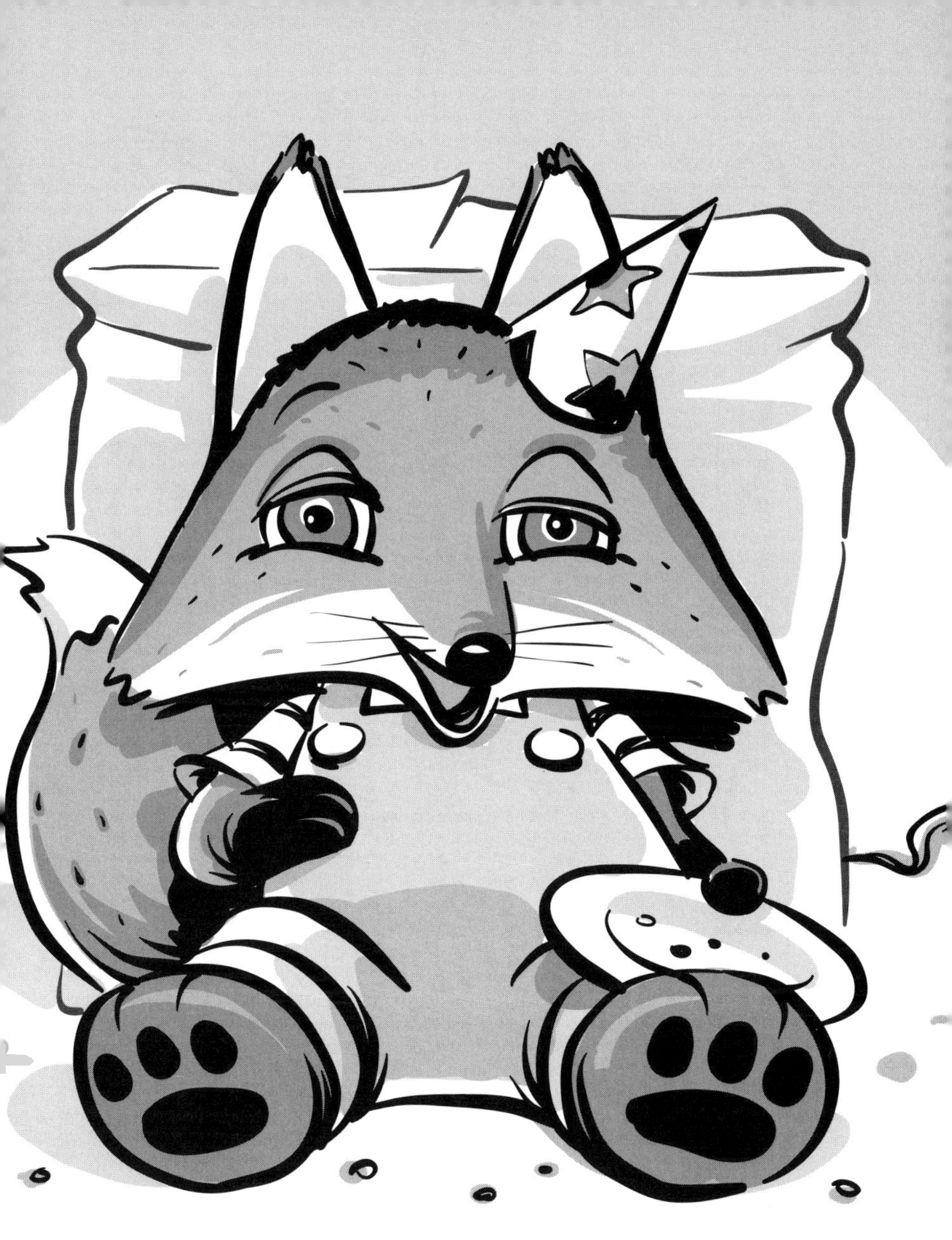

Fox, Cat, and Pig eat
a lot of cake.

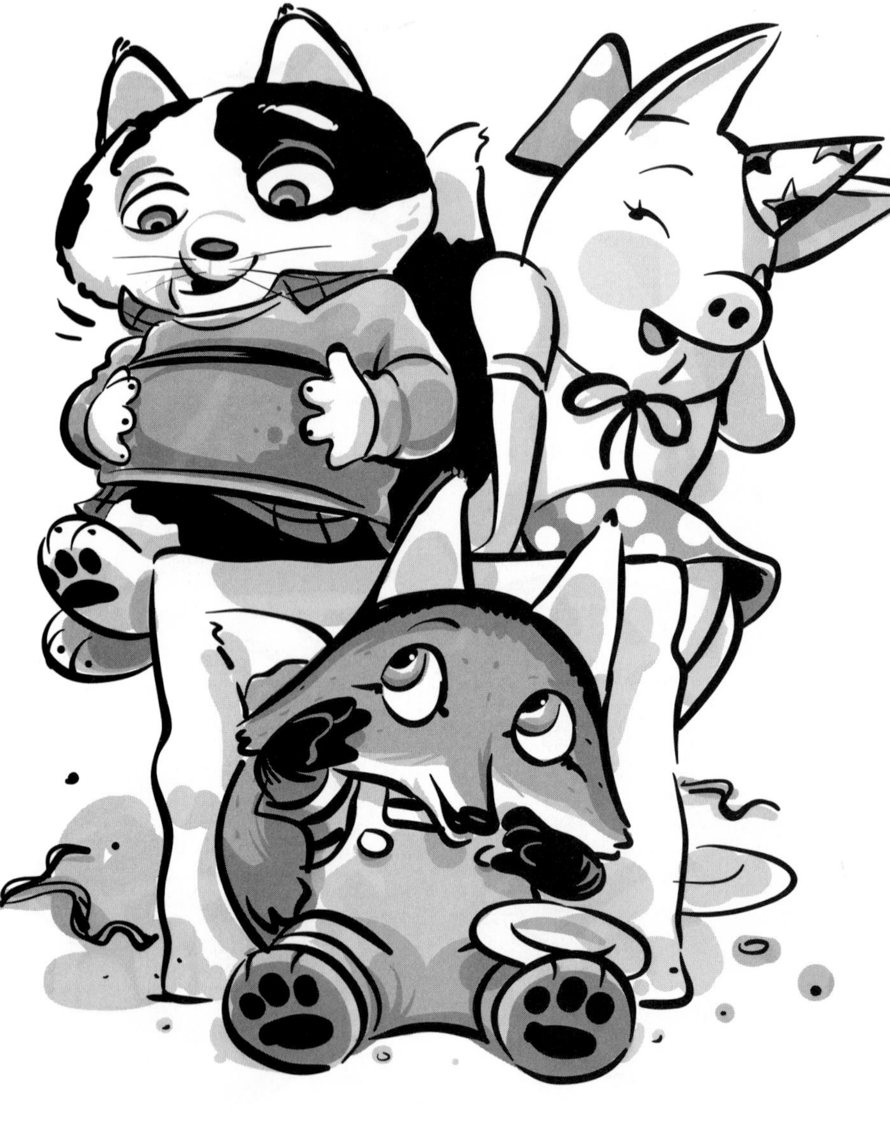

"No more!" says Cat.

"Not another bite!" says Pig.

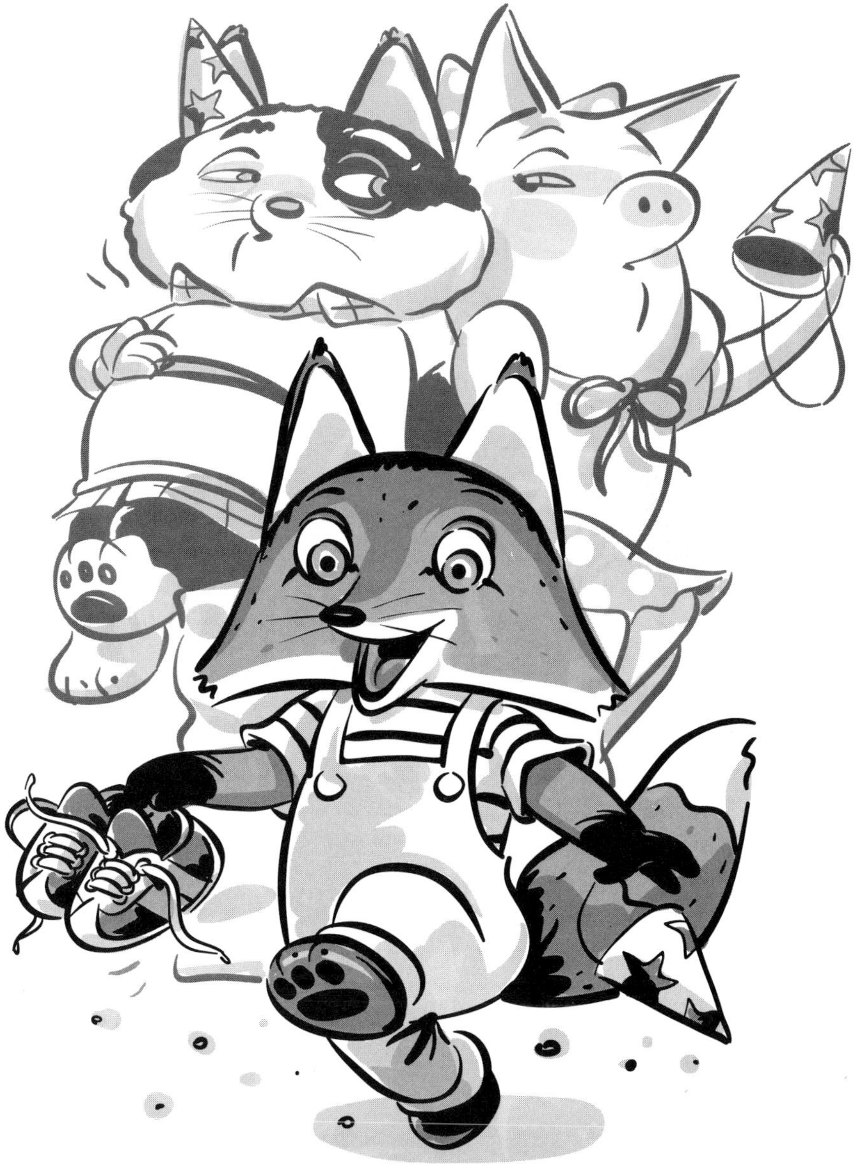

"Let's jog!" says Fox.

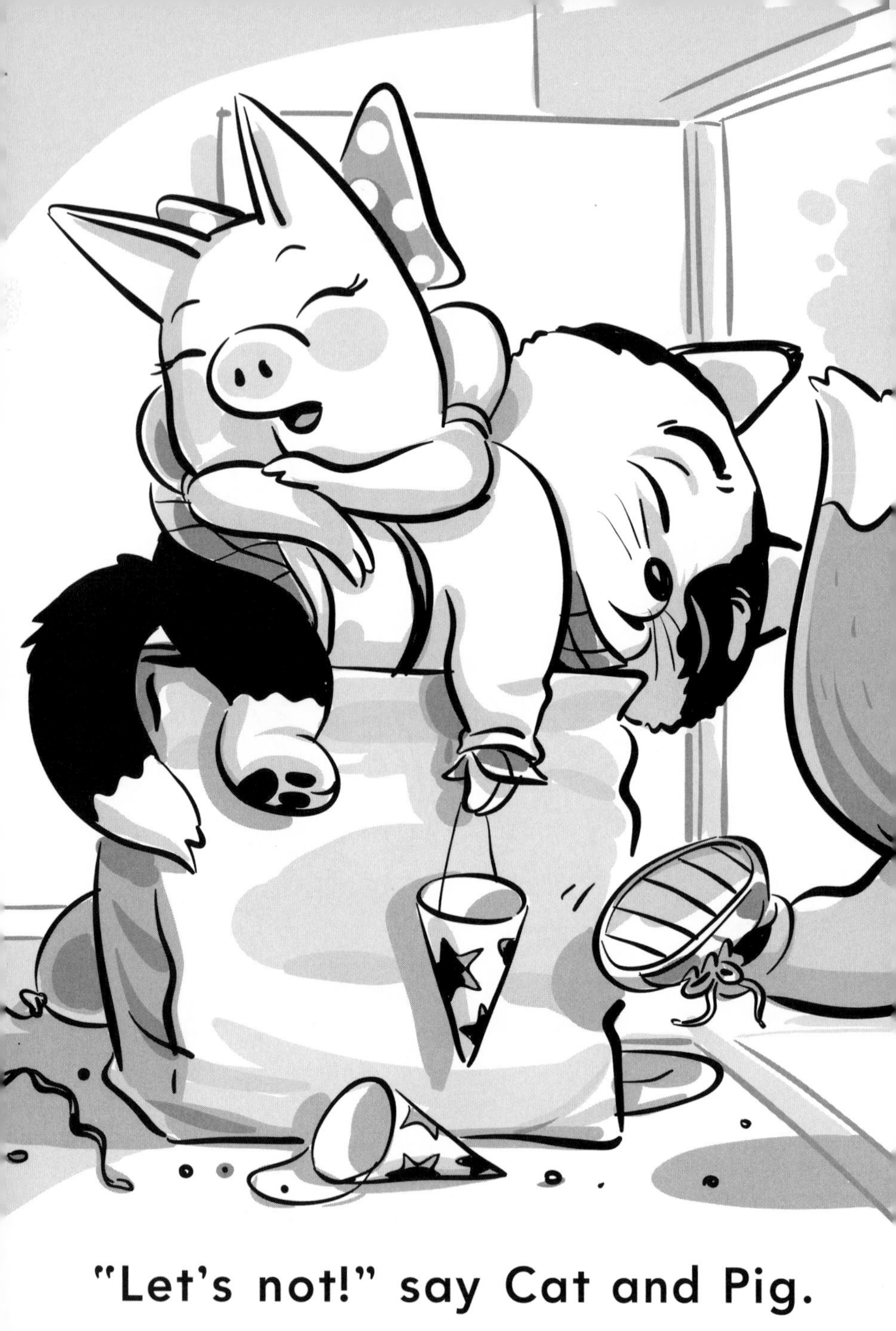

"Let's not!" say Cat and Pig.